Wright Brothers

Betty Lou Kratoville

ORDER DIRECTLY FROM
ANN ARBOR PUBLISHERS LTD.
P.O. BOX 1, BELFORD
NORTHUMBERLAND NE70 7JX
TEL. 01668 214460 FAX 01668 214484
www.annarbor.co.uk

Cover Design: Nanette Brichetto
Cover Photo: Pictorial History Research
Interior Illustrations: North Wind Picture Archives

International Standard Book Number: 1-57128-146-0

10 09 08 07 06 05 04 03
  1   0   9   8   7   6   5   4   3

Contents

CHAPTER 1

Early Days

Wilbur and Orville Wright loved to tinker! It began when they were very young. And it never stopped.

There is a famous tale about these two. Wilbur was eleven, and Orville was seven. One day their father brought an odd toy home. It was like nothing the boys had ever seen before. The toy was made of cork, paper, and a twisted rubber band. And it *flew*!

The brothers played with the toy for days. In

fact, they wore it out. They looked at the crumpled mass on the ground.

"Let's build a new one," said Wilbur. And they did. They built lots of new ones. Big ones. Small ones. For some reason, the small ones flew best. They never forgot that odd toy.

There is a word that best tells us about the Wright brothers. The word is *curious*. They were curious about everything. They wanted to know what made things work. They looked for answers. And then they used them.

They made their own wagons. Orville made a tool that would shape wood. Wilbur made a gadget to fold paper. Their father was a minister. He used Wilbur's machine to fold the church's newsletter each week. The boys built all sorts of kites. Theirs always seemed to fly better and higher than anyone else's. Now and then they would sell one of their kites. It meant a little extra spending money.

Folks always said that the brothers learned a lot of their skills from their mother. She was good at fixing things. She could make things, too. Once she made a sled. She gave it to her sons for Christmas.

Orville and Wilbur had two older brothers. They had one younger sister. None of them seemed to be "tinkerers."

Someone gave Orville a small printing press. He spent all of his spare time on it. He used it to print the school paper. He worked for a Dayton printer for two summers. Wilbur spent that time getting well. He had been hurt in an ice hockey game.

Not everything the boys tried worked. One day Orville made a batch of chewing gum. He used tar and sugar. Some of his friends tried it. They got sick! That gum was one of the brothers' few failures.

The time came for the brothers to set out to make their fortune. They both would have liked to go to college. But it was out of the question. There wasn't enough money. Also, they needed to stay close to home. Their mother had not been well for years. They wanted to be sure she had good care.

They had to find some way to earn a living. They began by building a printing press. It wasn't easy. They used old pieces of wood. They picked up iron in a junkyard. It turned out to be quite a good press.

How did they learn to do these things? They read. They read everything they could get their hands on. A new science book was always a treat. Sometimes they sent away for books. Other times they used the town library.

They used the press to print a weekly newspaper. Then a daily. Wilbur wrote all the stories. For a while it looked as if their printing press would be a success. But at that time there were four big daily newspapers in Dayton. These finally forced the brothers out of business.

What next? Bicycles had become very popular. Each of the brothers had one. Why not sell bicycles? Why not fix bicycles? Why not build bicycles? Why not all three? They named their business the Wright Cycle Company. And it was a great success.

Now what? Orville and Wilbur could not just sit back and enjoy their profits. They needed something new and exciting. Something that had a problem. Something that needed a pair of nimble brains. What about gliders? They had read about a man in Germany. He had made more than 2,000 glider flights.

The Wright brothers could not get gliders out of their minds. They searched for books about gliders. They thought about gliders. They talked about gliders. Soon it became clear. They would have to *build* a glider.

CHAPTER 2

Gliders

Books came in the mail from all over the country. Wilbur and Orville read every word. In this way they learned a great deal about flight. How men in other lands and at other times had wanted to fly. How foolish some of their efforts were. The brothers looked at one another and laughed at men who tried to copy birds in flight. These men tied wings to their legs and arms. Then they leaped from a high place. There were many broken bones and bashed heads.

The Wrights read about balloon flight. It was quite simple. Fill a huge balloon with hot air. Tie a basket to it. Put one or two people in the basket. Let it go. A thrilling ride but one had to go whichever way the wind blew. And sometimes the balloons landed in treetops or a lake.

As time passed, balloons grew larger. They were filled with gas. Someone thought of using a steam engine. Now the balloons could be steered just like a ship. And now they were shaped like a cigar.

One giant balloon even crossed the Atlantic Ocean. The people seemed to enjoy the flight. There were soft berths to sleep in. The meals were hot and good. There were card games to play and books to read. If one wished to smoke, one went into a small room with double doors.

Balloon flight seemed to be here to stay. England and Germany were in a race to see which country could build the biggest, safest balloon. But then as time went by, there were crashes. Quite a lot of crashes. Now and then a balloon caught on fire. People were killed. One terrible crash, the Hindenburg, shocked people all over the world. It was the end of travel by balloon.

It was time for the Wrights to learn as much as they could about gliders. They read about the German man named Otto Lilienthal. He was their hero. The wings of his glider were shaped like a butterfly.

Lilienthal had made dozens of short glider flights. Most of them were down hill. They lasted only a few seconds. But it was a start. The Wrights were stunned when they heard of his death. He died in a glider crash.

After Lilienthal's death, they read more. They worked harder. And they tried to judge the mistakes that had been made by others. There was so much to learn!

They saw that balance had always been a problem in gliders. Men had tried for balance by asking the glider pilot to shift his weight. Somehow this didn't make sense to Wilbur. He watched buzzards. They kept their balance by twisting their wing tips. Could a glider's wings be twisted the same way?

Their first try was part glider, part kite. It looked like a glider. But it flew like a kite. Ropes fixed to the wing tips controlled it well. That was only the start. The brothers built one glider after another. Each one was better than the one before it. Each one stayed in the air a bit longer.

Now they were ready. Orville wrote to the U.S. Weather Bureau. He wanted to know where the best place was to fly a glider. Kitty Hawk, North Carolina, said the experts. The winds there were strong. The land was flat and sandy. There were few trees.

Off to Kitty Hawk went the Wright brothers. They made more than a thousand glider flights there. Their flights were longer than any ever made before.

It was not an easy life. The brothers lived in a tent. Sometimes they had to hunt or fish for their supper. Yet they were content. They were busy. And they were doing what they most enjoyed – tinkering!

CHAPTER 3

The First Flight

The Wrights spent three summers at Kitty Hawk. They had made many changes in their glider. They made the wings longer. They added a tail. Now it seemed to fly just the way they wanted it to. All it needed for *powered* flight was a small motor. The motor would drive the plane through the air with a propeller. With enough speed, the air pressure below the wings would become greater than that above. The air below would push the plane up. At least that is what the brothers hoped would happen. Of course, it had never happened before. But why not?

They went home to Dayton. They made up their minds to spend a year in their lab. They needed to know many things. What was the best shape for a wing? How heavy could the motor be? What was the right size for the propeller? Should there be one propeller or two?

To find some answers they built a wind tunnel. A big fan drove air through the tunnel at 30 miles an hour. More than a hundred wings were tested in that tunnel. It was slow, boring work, but it had to be done.

Orville said, "I think we know more about curved wings than anyone else in the world of flight." And today we know he was right!

Time was important. Another man, Samuel Langley, was working on a plane. Wilbur and Orville read all about him in the newspapers. At last Langley thought his machine was ready to fly. It was launched from a floating catapult. It nose-dived straight into the Potomac River. The Wrights still had a chance to be first.

In September 1903 the Wrights took their flying machine to Kitty Hawk. They had to move it in parts. It was a biplane. (That means it had two wings.) It also had a name. They called it Flyer.

At last on December 14 Flyer was ready. The Wrights ran up a flag. This was a signal. It told

A crowd came to watch. Some came to jeer and laugh. Others came with high hopes.

friends that the first flight was about to take place.

A crowd came to watch. Some came to jeer and laugh. Others came with high hopes. Wouldn't it be great if the Wright brothers had made a machine that could fly! The brothers tossed a coin to see who would be first to fly the machine. Wilbur won the toss. He climbed into the plane. He lay down on his stomach.

The plane rushed down a small track in the sand. Up into the air it went. The onlookers held their breath. Then Wilbur made a mistake. He tried to turn the plane upward too fast. The engine quit. Down came Flyer after only three and a half seconds of flight.

There was some damage to the plane. It took three days to fix it. Now it was Orville's turn. He climbed into the plane. He warmed up the engine. Slowly the plane began to move. Wilbur ran alongside. Suddenly it rose. Flyer stayed in the air only 12 seconds. It went only 100 feet. But at long last – a powered flight!

The brothers made three more flights that day. Wilbur made the longest. He stayed in the air 59 seconds. The plane flew 852 feet. Onlookers cheered. Most of them could not believe their eyes. They were seeing the start of a new era in the history of the world!

The Wrights would have laughed at this. They did not see what they had done in that way.

They were modest men. But they did send a telegram to their father. It read:

Success! Four flights against wind with engine power alone. Average speed 31 miles. Longest flight 59 seconds. Inform press. Home Christmas.

CHAPTER 4

Work – and More Work!

"Inform press." Mr. Wright tried very hard to do what his sons had asked in their telegram. But the men who wrote for the newspapers didn't believe him. A machine that flies through the air? Nonsense! One or two papers printed a couple of lines. But their readers made fun of these reports. How could a couple of men who made bicycles build a machine that flew?

Wilbur and Orville went back to Dayton. There was work to be done. They built a new workshop and a hangar. They rented a pasture near Dayton. Here they tested Flyer II in May 1904. (They had to move the cows out of the way first!) It was a windy day. The motor had problems. The test failed. Once again the newspapers made fun of them.

The brothers were too busy to read the paper. In the next few years they made almost 400 flights. Each flight was just a little better than the one before. Wilbur made one flight in Flyer III that lasted 38 minutes! He could have stayed up longer but he ran out of gas.

People who lived nearby used to watch the flights in wonder. They feared these young daredevils would kill themselves. They stood by with first-aid kits in case there was a crash.

Things changed a lot after Wilbur's 38-minute flight. Now the newspapers hailed this great invention. People read about it. They came from near and far to watch the flights. One of the planes the brothers built had an open cockpit. It held two passengers. They gave rides to men brave enough to risk their lives. There was always great relief when the plane came down in one piece!

At this time Wilbur and Orville were waiting for a patent. Until they had one, anyone could copy their plane. They would not let photos be taken of Flyer III. When the plane was not in use, it was always locked safely away.

While waiting, they wrote to the British, American, and French governments. They said they were willing to sell Flyer III. They pointed out its great value. It could be used in war. It could carry mail. No reply came from the British. And the Americans! They would not even believe there was such a thing!

At last the French came through. They asked the Wrights to bring a plane to France. It would have to be tested there. Wilbur wasted no time. He sailed for France in May 1907. He would have to answer doubts that had been printed in a Paris newspaper.

The Wrights have flown or they have not flown. They have a machine or they do not have one. They are in fact either

flyers or liars. It is difficult to fly; it is

easy to say 'we have flown.'"

Ask your questions. Wilbur Wright would

soon be there!

CHAPTER 5

The Wrights in Europe

Wilbur's ship docked. He went straight to the French town of Le Mans. The Type A Flyer III was stored in a car factory. It had been there for almost a year. No one had taken care of it. So it was not in good shape. Wilbur worked hard on it for two months. Meanwhile the French kept on wondering. Would this odd machine ever get off the ground?

At last in August Wilbur said he was ready. A large crowd gathered at a racetrack in Le Mans.

Men had been hard at work on flying machines in other places. They were there that day. By now these men were called aviators. The aviators were not selfish. They had high hoped that the American plane would fly. But they were far from sure that it would even get off the ground. Too many times their own efforts had failed.

After noon Wilbur took off. He flew his plane in two wide circles. Then he gently landed it on the track. The crowd cheered. They tossed their hats into the air. The French aviators were thrilled.

"We are beaten," they cried. But they didn't seem to care.

Wilbur stayed in Le Mans for five more

Wilbur in France

days. In this time he made nine flights. Then he moved on to an army camp grounds. Things seemed to get better and better. In the next few months he made more than a hundred flights. On New Year's Eve he flew 2 hours, 20 minutes, and 23 seconds. This flight won him a prize of $4,000.

Crowds flocked from all over Europe. Everyone wanted to see this amazing flying machine. Now and then Wilbur took up passengers. One passenger was a woman. Before they took off, she tied her skirts around her ankles with a string. When she landed, she said it was the thrill of a lifetime!

Wilbur Wright was a mild fellow. He got on

well with most everyone. But there was one thing he would not do. He would not make a speech. He was often asked to do so. His answer was, "I know of only one bird that talks. It is the parrot. And it can't fly very high!"

While Wilbur was in Europe, Orville went to the East Coast. He took one of the Type A planes to Fort Myer. This fort was near Washington, D.C. He was to test fly the Type A plane for the U.S. Army.

Once again there were cheers and clapping at the end of the first flight. He made 10 flights on this trip. He stayed up for more than an hour in four of these flights.

The army was pleased. But they raised one

point. They wanted the plane to fly at a speed of 40 miles per hour. Orville thought longer propellers might add to the plane's speed. He changed the propellers.

A young army officer asked to go along on the next flight. That was all right with Orville. They had often taken passengers on their flights. During the flight the new propeller blade cracked. It cut a rudder wire. The plane plunged to the ground. Orville was badly hurt. He had a broken hip, leg, and ribs. The young officer died a few hours after the crash. He was the first person to be killed in an airplane crash.

When Orville was well, he joined Wilbur in France. Their sister went with him. Wilbur had been busy. He taught a group of French aviators to fly. He got a contract to build planes for the French army.

Next he went to Italy. There he was asked if he would teach some Italian army officers. Wilbur was a good teacher. It was a joy to him to pass on what he knew to others.

The Wright family had a grand time in Europe. They met heads of state. They met kings and queens. They stayed in beautiful homes. They were honored at fancy dinners. What fun after all the years of hard work! How nice no longer to be thought of as "crazy." The great respect and high praise were unlike anything they had ever known. But they seemed to handle it well.

At last it was time to go home. A grateful country was waiting to give them a warm welcome.

CHAPTER 6

Great Events

The age of flight had arrived. It grew by leaps and bounds. Men in the United States and in Europe worked to make planes better. It wasn't a race. These men wanted machines that would fly higher and faster. They wanted to be sure planes were safe. No one was quite sure how far this idea of flight would go. Would this machine be used for war or for peace? Would it last or would it fizzle out as balloon flight had done? Most men were pinning their hopes on flying machines being here to stay.

The world of aviation was waiting for an event planned for July of 1909. There was to be a contest. The first man to fly across the English Channel would win a large cash prize. The flight would start in the French town of Calais. It would end at the English town of Dover.

Two men made up their minds to try. One was a Frenchman, Louis Bieriot. The other was an Englishman, Hubert Latham. Latham took off first. His engine sputtered and stopped. The plane dived into the sea. Latham was lucky. The plane floated. He sat on top of it until a ship picked him up.

He planned to try again. But Bieriot was too

sly. He took off at night. That flight turned into a nightmare! A thick mist closed in. He could see nothing. He wished he could turn around and go back to France. But he did not know which way he was flying. Then a close call! He almost crashed into the white cliffs of Dover. At last he found the air field. It was a very tired, shaky young man who landed in that field But the prize was his!

A few years later two brave men decided they would try to fly across the Atlantic Ocean from Newfoundland to Ireland. They, too, flew blind through thick fog almost all the way. They did land safely – in a swamp!

All this time the Wright brothers were busy. Orville kept working with the army. He built a new plane at their small plant. This plane seemed to suit the army. They bought it for $30,000. Orville then went to Germany. He trained two aviators there and took a prince for a ride!

Wilbur came home from Europe. He was paid a huge fee to fly around the Statue of Liberty. Thousands of people watched in wonder. He also found time to train the first two American aviators. Until then he and Orville were the only pilots in the United States.

Both brothers worked on forming the Wright Company. This company built their planes. It kept their patents safe. It was Orville's job to train

*Wilbur was paid a huge fee to fly
around the Statue of Liberty.*

pilots. These men would then fly all over the country. They showed people how to fly planes. They took them up for flights. It was the best way to sell an airplane. Business was very good.

Next the brothers started a flying school. They put it in the old cow pasture where Flyer II had been tested so many years ago. Students came from all over the country.

On May 25, 1910, the brothers made their only joint flight. Orville was at the controls of the plane during this flight. Later Orville took his father up for a ride. Mr. Wright was then 82 years old.

"Higher, Orville, higher!" he cried.

Mr. Wright was often asked about his sons.

"Who did the most work?" people wanted to know. His answer: "About equal credit is due to each." The brothers looked alike, thought alike, and worked alike. They were a team in every way. As far as anyone knew, a cross word never passed between them.

"They are like twins," their father said.

CHAPTER 7

Final Flight

Wilbur died in 1912 of typhoid fever. Orville was broken-hearted. It helped to keep on working. Through the years he was often sad about the many things Wilbur was missing.

He missed the flights of Amy Johnson. Amy was a typist from a small English town. She fell in love with flying. She flew solo from England to Australia. It took her 19 days! A year later she flew to Japan. On this trip she had to fly across bleak Siberia. No towns or people for thousands of miles. Her next flight was to South Africa. All this not too many years after Wilbur had stayed aloft for 59 seconds!

Wilbur missed the great work of young Alan Cobham. Cobham made airline travel possible. He explored routes around the world. He searched out strips where airliners could land. He studied air currents and storm tracks. He made lots of notes on climate and weather.

He missed the 1920s. This is when the first airliners were built. Huge planes began to fly people and cargo.

Wilbur missed Lindbergh's solo flight in May 1927. Lindbergh was the first man to fly nonstop across the Atlantic Ocean. His plane, The

Spirit of St. Louis, was a monoplane. That meant only one engine. Had that engine quit, the plane would have dropped into the ocean.

Now and then Lindbergh would feel sleepy. He flew his plane as close to the water as he dared. Drops of water splashing from the waves helped to keep him awake. The world cheered this brave young man.

Wilbur also missed Amelia Earhart. She was the first *woman* to fly the Atlantic. This was five years after Lindbergh's flight. Planes had been greatly improved. But it still was a fearless thing for this young woman to do. And it was her flight that caused airlines to begin flying passengers across oceans.

Orville lived until 1948. He was able to enjoy all these wonders. Today the world takes flying pretty much for granted. But think about it! We sit in a soft seat 35,000 feet above the Earth. We sip a cold drink. We eat a hot meal. We watch a movie. We've come a long way since Flyer I lifted off the ground. And it all began with two brothers and their toy made of paper and a rubber band.